Geothermal Energy
AND Bio-energy

Julie Richards

This edition first published in 2004 in the United States of America by Smart Apple Media.

Smart Apple Media
1980 Lookout Drive
North Mankato
Minnesota 56003

Library of Congress Cataloging-in-Publication Data

Richards, Julie.
   Geothermal energy and bio-energy / Julie Richards.
   p. cm. — (Future energy)

Includes index.
Summary: Describes how heat beneath Earth's surface and plants and animals can be used as sources of power, how using this power affects the environment, and what the future significance of geothermal power and bio-energy may be.

ISBN 1-58340-336-1
1. Geothermal engineering—Juvenile literature. 2. Geothermal resources—Juvenile literature. 3. Biomass energy—Juvenile literature. [1. Geothermal engineering. 2. Geothermal resources. 3. Biomass energy. 4. Renewable energy sources.] I. Title.
TJ280.7.R52 2003
333.8'8—dc21   2002044636

First Edition
9 8 7 6 5 4 3 2 1

First published in 2003 by
MACMILLAN EDUCATION AUSTRALIA PTY LTD
627 Chapel Street, South Yarra, Australia 3141

Associated companies and representatives throughout the world.

Copyright © Julie Richards 2003

Edited by Anna Fern
Text and cover design by Cristina Neri, Canary Graphic Design
Illustrations and maps by Nives Porcellato and Andy Craig
Photo research by Legend Images

Printed in Thailand

Acknowledgements

The author and the publisher are grateful to the following for permission to reproduce copyright material:

Cover photograph: crop of sunflowers, courtesy of Corbis Digital Stock.

S. Aitzetmuller—OSF/Auscape International, p. 26; Y. Arthus-Bertrand—HoaQui/Auscape International, p. 16; John Cancalosi/Auscape International, p. 30; Martyn Chillmaid—OSF/Auscape International, p. 22; Kevin Hamdorf/Auscape International, p. 8; PH Renault—HoaQui/Auscape International, p. 19; Rob Walls/Auscape International, p. 29 (top); Australian Picture Library/Corbis, pp. 12, 14, 21, 25, 28, 29 (bottom); Coo-ee Picture Library, p. 10; Corbis Digital Stock, pp. 1, 24; Getty Images, pp. 5, 9, 13 (top), 17; Lineair, p. 11; Photolibrary.com, pp. 4, 20; Reuters, pp. 7 (top), 18 (top), 23.

While every care has been taken to trace and acknowledge copyright, the publisher tenders their apologies for any accidental infringement where copyright has proved untraceable. Where the attempt has been unsuccessful, the publisher welcomes information that would redress the situation.

Contents

Glossary words
When a word is printed in **bold** you can look up its meaning in the glossary on page 31.

What is energy?

Energy makes the world work. People, plants, and animals need energy to live and grow. Most of the world's machines are powered by energy that comes from burning coal, oil, and gas. Coal, oil, and gas are known as fossil fuels. Burning fossil fuels makes the air dirty. This is harmful to people and damages the environment.

Scientists are not sure how much longer fossil fuels will last. It depends on whether or not new sources of this type of energy are found and how carefully we use what is left. Scientists do know that if we keep using fossil fuels as fast as we are now, they *will* run out. An energy source that can be used up is called non-renewable. A renewable source is one that never runs out. The world cannot rely on fossil fuels as a source of energy for everything. We need to find other sources of safe, clean, renewable energy to power the machines we have come to depend on.

These are the fossilized remains of a fish. Fossil fuels are the plants and animals that died millions of years ago and turned into coal, oil, and gas.

Geothermal Energy
AND
Bio-energy

The Earth as a source of energy

The Earth is a source of different types of energy. Some types of energy are produced by the plants and animals that live on the surface of the Earth. Another type of energy comes from changes that happen deep inside the Earth. Energy that comes from the heat beneath the Earth's surface is called geothermal energy. On the surface of the Earth, plants and animals produce another type of energy known as bio-energy. Both are renewable sources of energy.

Heat from inside the Earth is released through holes and cracks in the ground.

Fact file

Geothermal comes from two ancient Greek words, *geo* meaning "Earth" and *therme* meaning "heat."

The trees burning in this forest fire are releasing their bio-energy as heat and light.

Where does geothermal energy come from?

Geothermal energy is heat stored within the Earth. At the center of the Earth is a core of **molten** metal. The temperature here is at least as hot as the surface of the Sun. This is hot enough to melt the surrounding rock, turning it into a thick, gluey porridge called **magma**. Heat moves from the core to the Earth's surface, heating the underground rocks as it passes through them. When the heat reaches the surface, it is carried away into space. We do not notice geothermal heat because the Sun has a more powerful heating effect on the surface than the Earth's core does.

Sometimes, geothermal energy heats underground water until it turns into steam. The steam bursts through a crack or hole in the Earth's crust as a geyser or hot spring.

The Earth is made up of a crust, a mantle, and a core.

Crust
The Earth's crust is made of cold rock between 4 and 45 miles (6–70 km) thick. The thinnest parts are beneath the sea.

Mantle
The mantle is made of thick, gluey magma and is about 1,900 miles (3,000 km) thick.

Outer core
The metal outer core is about 1,500 miles (2,300 km) thick.

Inner core
The metal inner core is about 1,500 miles (2,300 km) thick.

Where does bio-energy come from?

Bio-energy is made from biomass. Biomass is another name for plants and animals. Bio-energy can come from the **fermentation**, decay, or burning of plant and animal material. All living things need energy to grow and stay healthy. Animals and people get their energy from food. The plants which animals and people eat get their energy from the Sun.

When plants and animals die, what they are made of breaks down and changes into something else. This is called decay. **Microbes** make this change happen. When plant material is eaten, decays, or is fermented or burned, energy is released.

This woman is carrying blocks of dried animal droppings, which will be burned as fuel.

Fact file

Plants are nature's best and biggest stores of energy. Every year, plants store about 10 times as much energy as the human population uses.

Sun

The plant changes sunlight into food.

Plant-eating animal eats the plant.

Meat-eating animal eats the plant-eater.

Plants store energy from the Sun. The Sun's energy is passed along the food chain, giving energy to living things.

Using geothermal energy

Natural geothermal energy has many uses.

- It is used for heating and hot water and to generate electricity to power homes and industry.

- People use natural geothermal energy when they bathe in hot springs. Some people believe that bathing in the warm water and breathing the **vapors** from a hot spring can cure some diseases and relieve painful swollen limbs.

- The thick mud that spits and burbles near a hot spring is sometimes used as a face cream to help keep the skin soft and free of wrinkles.

The soil around some volcanoes is so full of goodness that many farmers can grow three crops a year instead of one. The goodness is contained within the molten rock that flows from the volcano.

Using bio-energy

Natural bio-energy is used by many gardeners. Decaying plant material, called compost, is stored in piles or containers. Compost is used to nourish the soil. As it decays, it gives off heat and moisture. It can be placed around the stems of young plants to protect them from frost, or to keep them moist during hot, dry weather.

Electricity

Natural energies are not always available or **convenient** to use. Electricity is the most convenient source of energy to be discovered. Electricity has powered the world's machines for the last 120 years.

Geothermal energy and bio-energy are safer, cleaner sources of renewable energy. Scientists have found ways to collect and use geothermal and bio-energy, and change them into electricity and fuel to keep the hungry machines running.

Before electricity, the fatty waxes and oils from the bodies of whales were used as biofuels. These fuels were burned in oil lamps or made into candles.

Geothermal energy through history

In ancient times, geothermal energy was difficult to **harness**. People mostly made use of it through hot springs.

Ancient use of geothermal energy

From 27 B.C. to A.D. 300, the Roman Empire stretched across many parts of the world. Bathing was an important part of Roman life, and the Romans built many baths in the cities they settled. Water that bubbled up from underground hot springs was used to fill baths as big as swimming pools. Some of the hot water vapor was piped under the tiled floor around the bath so that everyone could keep warm.

Modern use of geothermal energy

When machines were invented, they were powered by steam. The steam came from water which was heated by burning wood or coal. The steam from geysers could not be used because it was not a steady supply. It was not until 1903 that the world's first geothermal power station was built at Larderello, in Italy, on the site of ancient Roman baths. In 1904 it began producing electricity. The power station still operates today and produces enough electricity to power a small village. Today, in Iceland, the city of Reykjavik is one of the most pollution-free cities in the world because geothermal energy is used to heat most of its buildings.

Geothermal Energy AND Bio-energy

The city of Bath, in England, was named after the baths built by the Romans using the hot springs beneath the city. The baths are still used today.

Bio-energy through history

People have been using bio-energy to fuel their fires for thousands of years.

Ancient use of bio-energy

Wood was an extremely important source of bio-energy for many people, who used fire to cook food and to warm themselves. In the past, there were more forests and fewer people using those forests. Often, enough wood could be collected from the forest floor without chopping down trees. People who lived in areas with few trees would burn **peat** or the dried droppings of animals.

Modern use of bio-energy

Wood was the first fuel burned to heat the boilers in steam-powered machinery. The machines were kept near forests. As the forests were cleared, it took longer to bring wood to the machines. Coal was found to be a better source of energy than wood because it burned hotter and longer. There was plenty of coal in the ground, and machines were kept in factories as close to the coalmines as possible.

Peat

Burning peat as a fuel has been known since Roman times. In 1914, Russia opened the first peat-burning power station. Today, peat is burned in power stations in places where other fuels are in short supply, such as Finland, Russia, and the Irish Republic. Fuels such as peat, which are made from biomass, are called biofuels.

Fact file

Candlenuts were collected and used as candles by early settlers in Australia. They would thread them on wire and heat them. The nuts, which have oil inside them, would burn like candles.

Even today, in some countries wood is still the most important form of bio-energy.

Harnessing geothermal energy

Only a few places in the world use geothermal energy—Iceland, New Zealand, Japan, China, the Philippines, and parts of Europe, Africa, and the United States. The equipment needed to find and make use of geothermal energy is very expensive. The deeper within the Earth the hot rocks and water are, the harder it is to reach them. Only wealthy countries in certain parts of the world are able to make the most use of this kind of energy. Many of these countries are close to places where the geothermal energy is just below the surface, or where it comes to the surface by itself.

In poorer countries that have good geothermal energy sources, richer countries are building geothermal power stations. Houses, schools, and hospitals are built for the workers who come from overseas to build the power stations. The local people in the towns and villages get to use these things too. All the new buildings need clean drinking water, proper toilets, and electricity. As most of the governments are too poor to set up proper supplies of electricity or clean drinking water for all the visiting workers, the wealthy countries pay for them. Building a big power station can provide jobs for some of the local people, too.

This man is cooking on a geothermal grill on the island of Lanzarote, in the Canary Islands, Spain.

Where geothermal energy is found

The Earth's crust does not fit tightly like a skin. It is broken into pieces called tectonic plates. If the world's oceans were drained away, the Earth's surface would look a bit like a giant jigsaw puzzle. Most of the world's geothermal energy finds its way to the surface on or near the edges of these plates. The Earth's crust is weaker here and is covered with cracks and holes.

The energy might bubble gently to the surface as hot springs and gurgling mud pools, or it could be as explosive as a geyser. When magma pours from a crack or hole in the ground, called a volcano, it can be seen how destructive and **unpredictable** geothermal energy can be. This can make collecting and harnessing the energy difficult. Some geysers are predictable. This sort of geothermal energy is easier to harness.

Old Faithful geyser, in the U.S., erupts every 37 to 93 minutes. About 10,000 gallons (40,000 l) of water shoots 170 feet (52 m) into the air.

Fact file

The heat inside the rock below the Earth's surface contains as much energy as all of the people in the world use in one year.

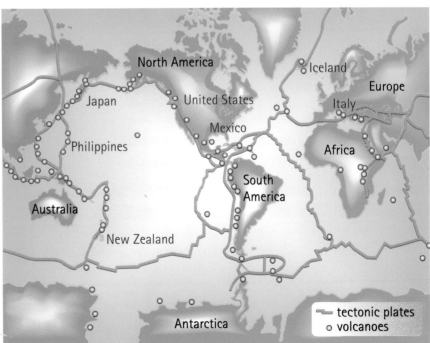

The Earth's crust is broken up into pieces. Most geothermal energy comes to the surface on or near the edges of these pieces.

North America
Iceland
Europe
Japan
United States
Italy
Mexico
Philippines
Africa
South America
Australia
New Zealand
Antarctica

— tectonic plates
o volcanoes

Modern geothermal technology

Scientists who study rocks and soil are called geologists. Geologists know where the weak spots are in the Earth's crust. They use photographs taken by **satellites** to help them work out how deep underground the energy is, and how hard it will be to cut through the rock to reach it.

Natural wells

Hot rocks lying a few miles below the surface can be reached by drilling a **well**. Underground water is heated as it passes through the cracks in the rocks. It collects in the bottom of the well and can be brought up to the surface.

Wells are drilled using a drill that has diamond teeth on a spinning tip. The wells are usually 1,000 to 10,000 feet (300–3,000 m) deep. It costs between one and four million dollars to drill each well, and most power stations have between 10 and 100 wells each. Drilling wells is the most expensive part of building a geothermal power station. Geothermal energy is usually found in very hard rock and this breaks the drill teeth. **Engineers** are trying to design better drills to save money.

A drilling rig drills into a thermal well for natural steam at a geothermal power station near Geyserville, California.

Human-made wells

If the hot rocks beneath the ground are dry, a human-made well can be created. Two holes are drilled some distance apart. Cold water is pumped down one hole. As water moves between the two holes, it is heated and is drawn out of the other hole as water or steam.

Explosives are used to shatter solid rock to allow the water through. High-pressure pumps force the water into the cracks in the rocks. Geothermal energy can heat water to 302 °F (150 °C) or more. Water that turns to steam is piped into a power station. When the heat is drawn from the steam, the steam **condenses** back into water. The cooled water is pumped back into the ground. Geothermal energy recycles the water to produce clean electricity.

Making electricity from geothermal energy

The pipe that pumps the hot water or steam up into the power station is higher than the pipe that pumps cold water down. This allows the water to stay on the hot rocks for as long as possible. Once it reaches the power station, the water or steam is passed through a **heat exchanger**. The heat energy is used to drive **turbines** that produce electricity.

If the water temperature is not high enough to produce steam straight away, the water is used to heat a second liquid that **boils** at a lower temperature than water. The vapor rising from this boiling liquid is used to drive the turbines to make electricity. Water that is almost steam is pumped into a special air tank that turns it into steam.

A geothermal power station pumps cold water onto hot rocks, turning it to steam.

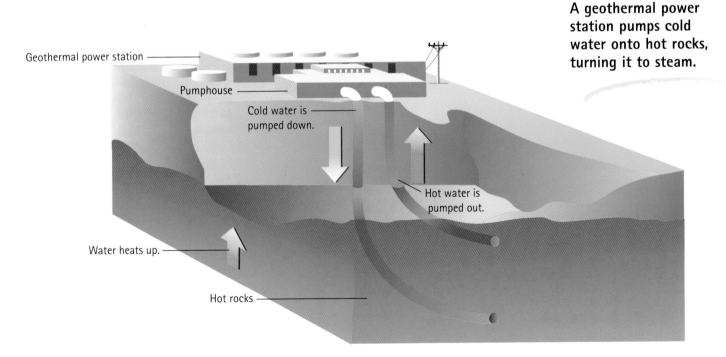

Geothermal power station

Pumphouse

Cold water is pumped down.

Hot water is pumped out.

Water heats up.

Hot rocks

Garbage being burned in an
incinerator at a Japanese garbage
disposal center. This heat energy
could be used to make electricity.

Making electricity from bio-energy

Biomass can be burned in power stations to make electricity in the same way that coal is burned. Some power stations burn woodchips and sawdust. Others burn the leftover stalks of wheat, barley, and oats. In some cities, landfill is burned in an **incinerator** to reduce the amount of space that garbage takes up. Rather than letting the heat escape through a chimney, it can be used to heat water to steam. In Sheffield, in the United Kingdom, landfill is burned to produce electricity and steam. The steam is made into hot water and piped to buildings, to be used as hot water or for heating. The incinerator burns at very high temperatures. This prevents poisonous gases from building up and escaping into the air. This is a much cleaner type of power station.

Waste

Steam is produced.

Electrical generator

Turbine

Electricity

Heat for drying waste

Waste is burned as fuel in furnace.

Waste can be burned to make electricity. The heat changes water to steam, which drives a turbine and electricity generator.

Geothermal Energy
AND
Bio-energy

Gasification—burning biofuels without pollution or waste

Oxygen makes the fuel in a fire burn hotter and faster. When fuel burns quickly, not all of it is converted to heat energy and a lot of thick, dirty smoke is produced. Conventional coal-fired power stations waste a lot of energy in this way. A lot of heat escapes into the air, as well as a lot of pollution.

Gasification is about controlling the amount of oxygen used during burning. If less oxygen is used, the fuel (both biofuels and fossil fuels) burns more slowly, and a clean gas is produced. Gasification uses fuel much more efficiently than a normal power station. More energy is drawn from less fuel and without a lot of pollution. Gasification is one way of obtaining more clean heat energy from existing supplies of wood, woodchips, and coal.

Scientists in Australia and the U.S. are developing a special gasifying generator that will burn wood slowly to produce lots more energy with less pollution. The generator will be built near large, fast-growing forests so that people in remote areas will have a steady supply of cheaper electricity.

Carbon dioxide from burning biofuels

Burning biomass does produce **carbon dioxide**. However, plants take carbon dioxide from the air and store it as energy. When plant material is burned, the amount of carbon dioxide returned to the air is small. When fossil fuels are burned, the carbon dioxide collected by plants over millions of years is suddenly released into the air in a very short time. Scientists think that all this carbon dioxide is trapping the Sun's heat and making the Earth warmer. This could change the world's weather and melt too much ice at the North and South poles. Low-lying countries might be flooded if melting ice raises the sea level.

Air pollution from burning fossil fuels damages the environment and people's health.

Biogas

Biogas is a mixture of methane and carbon dioxide. Biogas is made by letting microbes digest waste material. Methane gas trapped inside decaying garbage in a landfill can be released by drilling a well. The gas is piped to a power station where it is cleaned by special chemicals before being burned to make electricity.

Bio-digesters

A bio-digester is a large tank into which waste material such as droppings or food peelings can be emptied. Microbes inside it change the decaying waste material into methane gas that can be used for cooking, heating, and driving generators. Unlike coal, methane gas burns without creating any poisonous gases or particles that pollute the air.

Bio-digesters are perfect for remote areas where people are not connected to the main power supply. They can be set up easily and cheaply and solve the problem of what to do with animal and human waste. Containing waste in a bio-digester helps prevent the spread of dangerous diseases. Animal droppings have always been used as fuel, but they were often shaped into blocks by hand and left to dry in the Sun. Handling the droppings is not very safe or clean.

A small biogas digester in India. Animal dung is placed in the digester, where it decomposes and gives off methane gas. The gas is used as cooking fuel.

Geothermal Energy
AND
Bio-energy

A gasohol service station in Brazil. Gasohol is a mixture of gasoline and ethanol. Gasohol is a biofuel. Car engines have to be specially built or changed to run on this fuel.

Other biofuels

Biomass can be changed into liquid biofuels by fermentation. Sunflowers, sugarcane, corn, grasses, and many other plants can be turned into fuel for motor vehicles. Plants such as sunflowers have seeds that contain tiny amounts of oil which can be squeezed from them. Others, such as sugarcane and sugar beet, contain energy-rich sugars, which microbes can break down and change into a liquid called ethanol. Ethanol is mixed with **gasoline** to become bioethanol. Bioethanol can be used as fuel in cars.

Wood can be gasified. Wood is burned inside a special oven with very little oxygen. The wood burns hotter and the gases given off can be heated and changed into a liquid called methanol. Methanol can be mixed with oil from canola, soybean, and even animal fat to make biodiesel for trucks, oil heaters, and generators.

Biofuels do not cause pollution. As they can be made using many different plants, fuel can be made just about anywhere in the world. This would help many countries become less dependent on oil. Poorer countries that spend a lot of money on buying diesel to run generators could spend it on food instead. Energy crops would first feed the people. The leftover stalks and husks could then be burned to make electricity and fuel. Handling the waste could provide many people with jobs.

Fact file

When Henry Ford invented the first automobile, it was designed to run on ethanol. When Rudolf Diesel designed the first diesel engine, nearly a century ago, he ran it on peanut oil.

Geothermal energy at work

Although people still bathe in the water heated by hot springs, modern geothermal energy is mainly used to generate electricity.

Power stations

Most of the world's electricity is made inside power stations. Gigantic amounts of coal and oil are burned to heat water to steam. The steam spins turbines that power generators. The generators change the spinning movement into electricity. Power stations that burn coal and oil are using up a non-renewable source of energy. They are also causing terrible problems for the environment. A geothermal power station is using steam and hot water straight from the ground. There is no need to burn any fossil fuels. The water is a renewable resource that can be used again. Geothermal power stations need less looking after, too. Whereas other power stations make less electricity when equipment is being tested or repaired, geothermal power stations have fewer problems and are nearly always running properly.

This geothermal power station in Iceland uses geothermal energy to produce electricity.

The Geysers power station

The Geysers power station, in the U.S., is one of the few geothermal power stations in the world that uses scalding steam straight from underground to drive its turbines. The Geysers can supply as much power as two large coal- or nuclear-powered stations. It has 246 steam-producing wells and 14 wells where water is pumped back underground. The deepest well is nearly 2 miles (4 km) deep, and the steam travels through 55 miles (88 km) of pipes. To find out where the hot rocks are, holes are drilled and a special **probe** measures the temperature of the rocks.

Other uses for geothermal energy

The hot water from a geothermal power station has other uses. It can be piped to nearby buildings for heating and hot water. It can be piped to heat tanks in fish farms, dry crops, **pasteurize** milk in dairies, and heat greenhouses so that fruits such as bananas and mangoes can be grown in colder places. In countries where snow falls, it can be piped underneath roads and sidewalks to stop dangerous ice from forming. This makes driving and walking much safer during winter.

Some hot springs and geysers are very famous. Each year, thousands of people come to see them. These visitors need meals, places to stay, postcards, and **souvenirs**. Geothermal energy can be a useful source of wealth as well as energy for many towns and cities.

A thermal lake in Iceland. Pipes that carry hot water from geothermal sources are laid beneath roads in Iceland, to stop ice from forming on them.

Fact file

If all the geothermal energy sources in the U.S. were developed, they could supply 27 times the total energy used here every year.

Bio-energy at work

Energy crops

Many countries in the world are rich in biomass. Energy crops can be fermented into fuel for cars. What is left can be put into bio-digesters to break down into burnable gases and oils. Many energy crops can also be harvested for food first, and the leftover stalks and husks can then be used as bio-energy. Much of the technology needed is inexpensive and could be set up near the town or village using the bio-energy. There would be no need to transport waste material, making bio-energy cheaper and easier to produce. This would help people in poorer countries to be less dependent on burning wood. Some villagers turn their wood into a fuel called **charcoal**. Charcoal is much lighter for people to carry, but a lot of the energy is lost when wood is turned into charcoal.

Planting forests of fast-growing trees can provide other biofuels. The trees will also keep the soil in its place and prevent it being washed or blown away. Gasifying the wood means less of these forests would need to be chopped down because more energy could be taken from the wood. Burning wood does cause some pollution. Gasification would clean the few gases produced by burning the wood before the gases were released.

Each sunflower contains a tiny amount of oil, but a large crop of thousands of plants contains enough oil to make biofuels.

Fact file

There are enough woody weeds in northwestern New South Wales, Australia, to make more than 1.8 billion gallons (7 billion l) of bioethanol.

Electricity from landfill

Landfill sites take about three years to begin producing methane gas, and go on doing so for up to 15 years. The world's largest power station to run off methane gas was recently opened in Los Angeles. A network of pipes carries the gas to fuel 50 small turbines that spin to generate electricity. The power station is hidden behind the hills and operates more quietly than a normal power station. The amount of poisonous gases it prevents escaping into the air is the same as taking 500 cars off the roads.

Hog power

In the Chinese village of Linchun, methane gas produced from hog droppings and rotted sugarcane is used to power street lights, stoves, and heaters. After the gas has been taken from the pits of rotting waste, the farmers use the leftover waste material as fertilizer for their crops. One family alone used to burn 2.2 tons (2 t) of firewood each year for cooking and heating. Since they have been using methane, the amount of wood burned has dropped to less than 110 pounds (50 kg).

Fact file

China is the most populated country in the world. In one part of China, more than a million methane pits have been in use since 1997. Another 300,000 are being built.

This well, in New Jersey, U.S., extracts methane gas from garbage buried in a landfill.

Geothermal energy and the environment

Geothermal power stations are kinder to the environment than normal power stations because they use a renewable energy source and produce little or no dangerous gases. However, there are some things that worry scientists.

- Taking large amounts of water from the ground might disturb the water table. The water table is the natural level of water in the ground. If too much water is taken, the level of the water table can fall, making the land shrink and sink. This is why geothermal power stations always pump the water they use back underground.

- Geothermal wells may dry up if so much energy is taken that water cannot return and be heated quickly enough to keep up the supply.

- Underground water often contains minerals and gases that are smelly or **corrosive**.

- The noise of steam being released from high-pressured tanks when they are cleaned is similar to that of a jet aircraft taking off.

Gases produced by geothermal energy can smell like rotten eggs.

Geothermal Energy AND Bio-energy

•26•

Bio-energy and the environment

Forests and peat **bogs** are disappearing all over the world. These kinds of bio-energy sources need to be carefully managed to make sure that the problems caused by overuse do not happen. More than half the people in the world rely on wood as their main source of energy. Forests must be replanted, and growing energy crops can help soil recover from over-clearing. Unfortunately, peat bogs are not as easily replaced. It takes thousands of years for peat to form and removing the peat destroys the bogs.

Global warming

Carbon dioxide is one of the greenhouse gases that contributes to **global warming**. Biomass releases carbon dioxide as it burns. Although this is harmful to the environment, burning biomass causes less damage than burning fossil fuels such as coal or oil. Living plants actually remove carbon dioxide from the air, helping to keep it fresh and clean. As the forests disappear, there are fewer plants to clean the air.

When fossil fuels are burned, they release back into the air all the carbon dioxide that has been locked away for millions of years.

In developing countries, wood is the main source of energy. As forests are cut down and not replaced, wood is becoming very difficult to find.

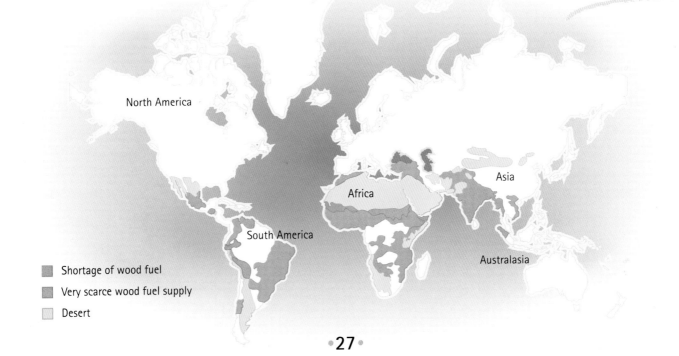

North America

Asia

Africa

South America

Australasia

■ Shortage of wood fuel
■ Very scarce wood fuel supply
□ Desert

Geothermal energy in the future

Countries with geothermal energy sources are beginning to understand that it might be better to spend money on developing this source of energy, rather than buying oil and coal from other countries. Only a few countries have oil to sell, and at times it is very expensive.

New technologies

Scientists in the U.S. are looking at creating human-made geysers in the same way that human-made geothermal wells are created. Scientists also know that some hot, dry rocks get their heat from **radioactive** minerals. Japanese and European scientists are finding ways that this energy might be collected and used to make electricity.

Really useful geothermal energy lies 5 to 10 miles (8–16 km) underground. At this depth, just about anywhere in the world, there are rocks hot enough to heat water past boiling point. Once drilling technologies have improved, geologists hope to be able to drill down to that depth and pump cold water in one well and then draw off the heated water from another well. A source of renewable energy like this would end the world's reliance on fossil fuels.

Fact file

In Japan, the water from a hot spring at Beppu is so hot that people can hard-boil eggs in it.

This rocky land on the Spanish island of Tenerife, is made of cooled magma. The hot magma has gone back underground and is too deep to be useful as geothermal power.

Geothermal Energy
AND
Bio-energy

Bio-energy in the future

Future bio-energy may come from the sea. Most of the Earth is covered by water. Seaweed grows in shallow water around the continents. In the future, seaweed may be farmed as an energy crop and changed into fuel. Brown seaweed was grown on a huge web of cables in the sea near California in the U.S. It was harvested and processed into methane gas.

Seaweed may be a source of electricity in the future.

Flexible fuel vehicles

A special kind of car called a flexible fuel vehicle (FFV) is being developed to use biofuels. FFVs are already being tested and can run on gasoline or a mixture of gasoline and bioethanol. After 2005, there will be more FFVs, and some service stations will have pumps for biofuels and biogas. In 1992, more than 39 cities in the U.S. passed laws making drivers use a biofuel and gasoline mix when there is not enough wind to blow away city smog.

In the future, some cars may run on more than one source of energy. These are called hybrid cars. Some of these cars may use special **fuel cells**. A fuel cell produces energy through chemical reactions, like a **battery**. Fuel cells can use methane, methanol, or ethanol to produce electricity to power an electric motor instead of a gasoline engine. A fuel cell operates as long as fuel is fed continuously into it. Fuel cells will power ships at sea and perhaps even colonies in space.

Fact file
A thousand methane-producing landfills could produce enough electricity to power three million homes. This would lessen the same amount of pollution as removing 24 million cars from the roads.

This factory in Brazil turns sugarcane into a fuel that cars can use.

Advantages and disadvantages of geothermal energy and bio-energy

Fossil fuels are non-renewable sources of energy that are running out. If we keep using them at the current rate,

- coal will run out in 250 years
- oil will run out in 90 years
- gas will run out in 60 years.

There are other sources of energy that are cleaner, safer, and will not run out. Geothermal power and bio-energy are safe, clean, and renewable sources of energy for the world's future power needs.

Geothermal power and bio-energy can help solve many of the world's energy and pollution problems.

ADVANTAGES OF GEOTHERMAL ENERGY AND BIO-ENERGY	DISADVANTAGES OF GEOTHERMAL ENERGY AND BIO-ENERGY
• Geothermal and bio-energy are both sources of clean and safe renewable energy.	• Bio-energy produces some carbon dioxide, but not nearly as much as fossil fuels do. The extra energy crops that are grown soak up much of the carbon dioxide that is released during burning.
• Bio-energy uses the waste materials we are running out of space to store.	
• Bio-energy is useful for remote places and can be tailored for use in individual households (using, for example, bio-digesters, methane pits, and micro-turbines) as well as larger areas.	• Some smelly gases and noise are produced by geothermal power stations, but they are usually far from where people live.
• Geothermal power stations recycle water and are easy to look after.	

Glossary

acids a type of chemical that can be harmful to people and the environment

battery a container filled with chemicals that can store or produce electricity

bogs land that is wet and spongy

boils when a liquid is heated until it turns into a gas

carbon dioxide a colorless gas that is breathed out by humans and other animals

charcoal wood used for fuel that has been burned with very little air

condenses when a gas or vapor changes into a liquid

convenient easy to use

corrosive eats away metal

efficiently without waste

engineers people who design and build machines, roads, buildings, and bridges

fermentation the breaking down of a substance by tiny microbes, which gives off a gas

fuel cells devices that produce electricity from a continuous chemical reaction inside them

gasoline a liquid fuel made from oil that is burned inside an engine

generator a machine that turns energy into electricity

global warming a rise in the temperature of the Earth's surface caused by burning fossil fuels

harness to control and put to work

heat exchanger a device that takes heat from one place and sends it to another place

incinerator a furnace used to burn garbage

magma rock that has become so hot it has melted

microbes very small living things that can only be seen under a microscope

molten rock or metal that has melted into a thick, sticky liquid

oxygen a colorless gas that is breathed in by humans and other animals

pasteurize a heating process that kills the microbes living in milk

peat a spongy, dark-brown, decaying plant material found in cool, wet parts of the world, which can be dried and burned as fuel

probe an instrument used for measuring and examining

radioactive giving out invisible rays of energy and particles

satellites spacecraft that circle the Earth and send and receive information

souvenirs reminders of somewhere

turbines motors with wheels that spin when they are pushed by a stream of air, water, or steam

unpredictable not knowing if or when something will happen

vapors a collection of tiny droplets of water, like a mist

well a hole drilled into the Earth

Index

Geothermal Energy AND Bio-energy